CORTES
CONQUEROR OF
MEXICO

FERDINAN:CORTESIV

CORTES
CONQUEROR OF
MEXICO

by William Jay Jacobs

Franklin Watts
New York / Chicago / London / Toronto / Sydney
A First Book

Cover illustration by Amy Wasserman
Cover map copyright © North Wind Picture Archives, Alfred, Me.
Cover portrait courtesy of The Library of Congress
Map on page 21 courtesy of Gary S. Tong

Photographs copyright ©: Art Resource, NY: pp. 2 (Scala), 14 (Giraudon),
42 (Lauros-Giraudon); North Wind Picture Archives: pp. 10, 17, 23, 30, 34, 41,
47, 48, 50, 52, 56; Ancient Art & Architecture Collection: pp. 12, 25 top; Photo
Researchers, Inc./George Holton: p. 20; Robert Frerck/Odyssey/Chicago: pp. 25
bottom, 54; The National Geographic Society, painting by Ned M. Seidler: p. 28;
The Bettmann Archive: pp. 31, 38.

Library of Congress Cataloging-in-Publication Data

Jacobs, William Jay
Cortés, Conqueror of Mexico / by William Jay Jacobs.
p. cm.
Includes bibliographical references.
ISBN 0-531-20138-4
1. Cortés, Hernan, 1485–1547—Juvenile literature. 2. Mexico—History—Conquest,
1519–1540—Juvenile literature. 3. Conquerors—Mexico—Biography—Juvenile litera-
ture. 4. Governors—Mexico-Biography—Juvenile literature. [1. Cortés, Hernando,
1485–1547. 2. Explorers. 3. Mexico—History—Conquest, 1519–1540.]
I. Title. II. Title: Conqueror of Mexico.
F1230.C835J33 1994
972' .02'092—dc20   93-31177
[B]   CIP AC

CONTENTS

Gold! Gold! Gold! Gold!
Bright and yellow, hard and cold.

— THOMAS HOOD, *Miss Kilmansegg*

PREFACE

To the deeply religious Aztec Indians of Mexico, Hernando Cortés was not a Spanish adventurer greedy for gold. He was a god. Often lucky in his life, Cortés happened to march inland from the eastern sea in the very year that an ancient Aztec legend promised the return of a fair-skinned, bearded hero who once had lived among them. Instead of the return of a lost god, the coming of Cortés brought the fabulously wealthy Aztec civilization only death — and eventually destruction.

The conquest of Mexico by Cortés is one of history's great tales of personal courage and strength. With only a few hundred Spanish soldiers, the stouthearted conquistador, or conqueror, toppled the mighty Aztec empire. In less than three years, 1519 to 1521, he brought to its knees a North American civilization that was hundreds of years old, and replaced it with the European culture and the power of Catholic Spain.

At almost every step of the way, defeat seemed cer-

The Aztecs worshipped a number of gods in many different temples. Here the Aztecs make an offering to the sun.

tain for Cortés and his tiny army. Montezuma, emperor of the Aztecs, could call on thousands of warlike natives to crush the invaders. The Aztecs, who regularly sacrificed captives from neighboring tribes to their gods, took pride in cutting out the still-beating hearts of Cortés's followers and placing them on altars already stained with human blood. In the end, however, it was the Indians who perished, along with their incredibly beautiful city of silver and gold.

Who was this man Cortés? What drove him to the heights of courage and the depths of brutality for which he is remembered? And how did he manage to gain so remarkable a victory, one that changed the course of history?

*Gold was a powerful magnet that drew
Europeans to the Americas. This is a
pre-Columbian gold head made in Mexico.*

12

CHAPTER ONE
A
DREAM
OF
FAME AND FORTUNE

When the ships of Christopher Columbus first sighted land in the Western Hemisphere, Hernando Cortés was only seven years old. He had been born in 1485 in Medellín, a small town in Estremadura, Spain. As a child Cortés often was ill, but by the time he was fourteen his health was so much better that his parents sent him to school at the University of Salamanca, hoping he would become a lawyer.

Quick-witted and alert, Hernando proved to be anything but a scholar. He much preferred playing cards and dice, fighting, and learning the skills of warfare. Soon he became an excellent horseman and fencer. He could fire weapons accurately both on foot and on horseback. After only two years at the university, he left, returning home to Medellín.

The early years of the sixteenth century found the Spanish people bubbling with high hopes. It was a lively time for a teenage boy like Cortés, eager for ad-

Christopher Columbus Being Received
by Isabella the Catholic and Ferdinand
of Aragon *painted by Eugene Deveria*

venture and excitement. The marriage of Ferdinand and Isabella had united the nations of Aragon and Castile into the strong new nation known as Spain. The two monarchs eagerly threw their country into the race for world leadership. And, for a time, they were successful. The spectacular discoveries of Columbus gave Spain a head start in the Western Hemisphere. Spanish armies were victorious in Italy. The Spanish people began to think of themselves as a superior people — a people of destiny.

Young Cortés, without a job, dreamed of becoming a soldier and of making his fortune. In 1504, at the age of nineteen, he got his chance. As a member of a force of soldiers, he sailed to the port city of Santo Domingo on the Spanish-controlled island of Hispaniola, in the Caribbean Sea.

People who saw him there described Cortés as a slender, pale-skinned young man of medium height. His body was muscular and athletic. Although later in life he was pictured as very serious, at nineteen he laughed often and was popular for his charm and grace. Like many conquerors of history, he ate mostly simple foods, drank little, and needed little sleep. Even at nineteen, he had a burning desire for fame and fortune.

On his arrival in Santo Domingo, Cortés was given a grant of land with Indians to serve him. At first he was disappointed, declaring that he had come in search of

gold, not to farm the land like a peasant. The Spanish governor of Hispaniola, however, convinced him that it was important, first of all, to earn money. Searching for gold meant hiring soldiers and buying equipment, which was an expensive business. Cortés agreed to try. He settled down to running his estate and before long, he was rich.

In 1511, Cortés agreed to help Diego Velázquez in the Spanish conquest of Cuba. In battles there, he proved himself to be a brave, determined soldier. When Velázquez was named governor of Cuba he rewarded Cortés with an even larger grant of land and still more Indian slaves.

Cortés and Velázquez learned of a great civilization on the Yucatán Peninsula of Mexico, a society far more advanced than any on the islands of Hispaniola or Cuba. It was the ancient society of the Maya, a people who built many roads, aqueducts, and bridges and who had a calendar more exact than any in use at that time in Europe. Unlike other Indian peoples of the Americas, the Maya had a well-developed system of writing and were expert in science and mathematics. But there was something else that interested the Spanish explorers who first had come in contact with the coastal Indians in the Mayan territory. The people they met made ornaments from a variety of precious stones and pearls. They had works of art made of silver and of gold. More than

Diego Velázquez

anything else, it was just such wealth that the Spaniards truly craved. Velázquez decided to send an expedition to Yucatán, and as its commanding officer, he chose Hernando Cortés.

C H A P T E R   T W O
IN
SEARCH
OF
GOLD

The expedition was just the opportunity Cortés had wanted. In robust good health, ambitious, and always a gambler, he decided to risk everything on this one throw of the dice. To prepare for the adventure, he spent his own money to buy muskets, ammunition, crossbows, navigational instruments, and supplies. He gathered an army of Spaniards, promising his recruits boundless wealth in gold, land, and Indian slaves. When his own cash savings were spent, he borrowed from friends, and finally mortgaged his plantation.

In the middle of February 1519, he sailed with a fleet of eleven ships to an island off the coast of the Yucatán Peninsula. From there he launched his attack on the Maya. On board his ships were about one hundred sailors, five hundred soldiers, a few hundred Indian servants, ten large cannons, and four small field guns. Facing the Spanish force was the might of an ancient empire.

The fighting proved bloody, but the Spanish army,

Ancient Mayan ruins as they appear today

because of its muskets and crossbows, completely put down the Mayan Indians. Cortés's cavalry especially frightened the Indians who had never seen horses before. Believing that the horse and rider were one creature, they fled in terror.

After the fighting, the Mayans promised to obey Cortés. A group of Indian leaders brought him gifts of fruit and birds. Later, other Maya came with ornaments of gold.

Sailing westward along the Mexican Gulf coastline Cortés landed at a port he named Vera Cruz. There he

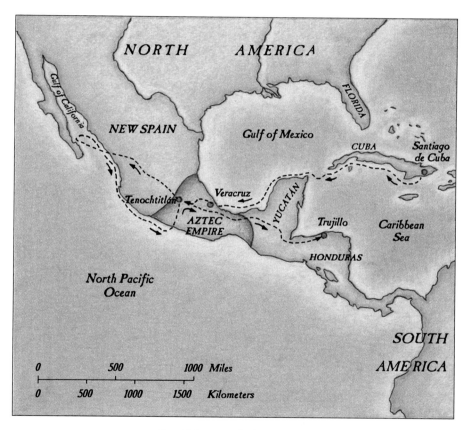

Cortés's travels in Mexico

was met by two Indians, ambassadors sent by Montezuma, the mighty leader of the Aztecs and ruler of most of Mexico.

Montezuma's spies had been closely following the progress of the Spanish fleet. Now, at their emperor's request, the two Indians brought the strangers from across the eastern sea a chest filled with handsome gifts. There were ornaments of gold and fine white cloth trimmed with golden feathers. There were rare foods.

Through Doña Marina, an Indian woman traveling with him, Cortés told the Indian ambassadors that he was eager to visit the city of Emperor Montezuma. When they hesitated, Cortés decided to show his power. He had his cavalry gallop at full speed across the beach. Then he fired his powerful, noisy cannons.

Cortés did not know it, but the Indians were already convinced of the white men's power. Like most of the Indian peoples, the Aztecs looked forward to the return of one of their gods, Quetzalcóatl. According to legend, that kindly god was fair-skinned and bearded. He once had lived among the Indians. Quetzalcóatl taught them to till the soil and gave them their calendar, and when he departed to lands beyond the eastern sea, he promised to return someday.

Montezuma was an Aztec priest and very superstitious. Just before the coming of Cortés he witnessed such strange signs as a comet in the sky, a fire in the holy temple, and voices wailing in the night. Then came

The Aztec emperor Montezuma

word of the "superhuman" Spaniards, who rode four-legged dragons and killed Indians from a distance with bolts of lightning and thunder.

What should Montezuma do? Should he resist Cortés and the Spanish army? Or should he receive them as gods? Truly he believed that Cortés was the "fair god" returning to his people. Yet, at the same time, he could not help but fear the strangers.

When Montezuma learned that Cortés was advancing toward his capital city, Tenochtitlán (now Mexico City), he sent new ambassadors to say that such a visit was impossible. This time the emperor's representatives brought to Cortés even richer presents than before: a disk of gold as large as a cartwheel and another even larger made of silver, beautifully molded golden articles in the shape of animals, and a war helmet filled with grains of gold.

Instead of convincing Cortés to leave Mexico, Montezuma's gifts only made the conquistador even more eager to reach the source of the spectacular wealth spread before him. This, he realized, would be the greatest chance for fame and fortune that he would ever have.

Still, there was a problem. Velázquez had never given Cortés permission to make war and to set up a Spanish colony in Mexico with Cortés as captain general. What Cortés was doing could be labeled as treason, and for that, he could be executed.

Meanwhile, some of the men in Cortés's army

Top: *The gold and wealth Cortés saw in Mexico
made him even more eager to make
it a Spanish possession.*

Below: *Mexican muralist Diego Rivera
painted this view of Tenochtitlán.*

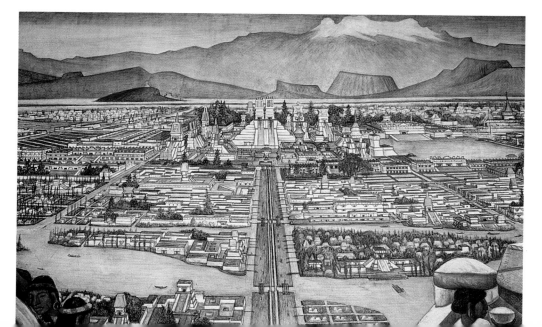

wanted desperately to return to Cuba. They feared that trying to conquer a mighty empire with only a handful of soldiers would mean almost certain death. Cortés acted with boldness. Secretly he ordered the sinking of every ship in his fleet. Then he told his men that the ships had been unsafe to sail. With no ships to carry them back to civilization, every man in the Spanish force knew that the only hope for survival was victory. As Cortés said to his troops, "We must look to God and to our own good swords and stout hearts."

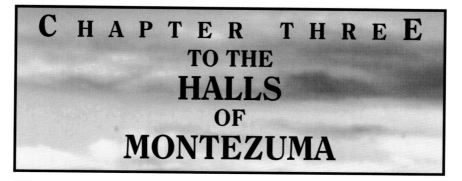

CHAPTER THREE
TO THE
HALLS
OF
MONTEZUMA

From Vera Cruz on the Mexican coastline to the Aztec capital city of Tenochtitlán was a distance of 275 miles (443 km). The pathway twisted and wound through thick forests and high mountains, a wilderness that was home to rattlesnakes, scorpions, poisonous ants, and jaguars. Also, barring the way for Cortés in the summer of 1519 were some of North America's shrewdest and best-trained warriors, the Tlascalan Indians. Before long some 50,000 Tlascalans gathered to face Cortés and his army of 400 Spaniards. A ferocious struggle began. Cortés's powerful cannons ripped great holes in the massed lines of Indians. His cavalry trampled the corpses. Finally, the Indians decided to surrender.

When the Tlascalans gave up, Cortés rewarded them richly with gifts. As he entered their capital city, the Indians kissed the ground where he was about to walk. They showered the Spanish soldiers with flowers and prepared magnificent banquets for them. Even

*Cortés and the Spanish battled
the well-trained Tlascalan Indians.*

more important, Cortés discovered that the Tlascalans deeply hated Montezuma and his tax collectors. They offered to provide Cortés with 10,000 warriors for his march to Tenochtitlán.

On November 1, 1519, the Spanish force began its

march through the beautiful countryside leading to the city of Emperor Montezuma. Seven days later they arrived at Tenochtitlán. The city stood on an island, close to the shore of Lake Texcoco. Other cities and smaller towns also were built both on the lake and on dry land nearby.

On first seeing the Aztec capital, the Spaniards were astonished. White towers and temples seemed to rise out of the water. Stone palaces with many spacious rooms spread out into great courtyards. Orchards and gardens, flowers and fruit trees were everywhere. There were tiled walkways and little ponds filled with ducks and fish. Canoes glided alongside the three broad causeways that linked the city to the shore. To Cortés and his men, Tenochtitlán, "the City of Mexico," was a place of enchantment, a fairyland of towers and water.

Mounted on horseback at the head of his army, Cortés slowly advanced along one of the causeways leading to the city. Throngs of curious Aztecs lined the roads to watch the strangers arrive. At one gateway, members of the Aztec noble class waited in silence to welcome the Spanish leader. As he approached, each noble in turn placed his hand on the earth and then raised it to his lips, kissing the ground in formal welcome to the Spaniards. Then, between two lines of colorfully dressed chieftains, came Montezuma himself, carried on a litter decorated with gold and silver trimming. The litter was covered by a canopy of green feath-

*The beauty and grace of the Mexican
capital, Tenochtitlán, captivated the Spanish.
Canoes linked the city to the shores of the lake.*

 30

*The Spanish conquistador Cortés
meets the Aztec emperor Montezuma.*

ers and set with pearls and glistening jewels. Even the
sandals on the emperor's feet were covered with precious jewels.

As Montezuma was lowered from his litter, Cortés
dismounted. Four Aztec lords respectfully placed cloths
on the ground for their emperor to walk upon. About

forty years old, tall and slender, Montezuma walked with great dignity toward the Spaniards.

Cortés waited for his friend and interpreter, Doña Marina, to stand next to him. Then, with his usual charm, he removed a necklace of pearls and glass beads that he was wearing and put it around Montezuma's neck.

Cortés and Montezuma said gracious things to each other. They walked together in a formal procession down the causeway, stopping at a large, handsome palace that had been made ready for Cortés and his troops.

That day, November 8, 1519, was to be the turning point in the long history of the Aztec people. Never again would their society be the same.

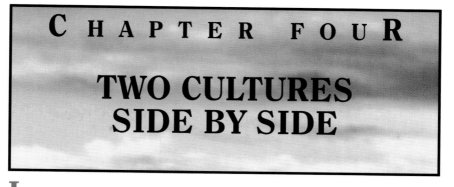

CHAPTER FOUR

TWO CULTURES SIDE BY SIDE

In the weeks following his arrival in Tenochtitlán, Cortés spoke often with Montezuma. Slowly a friendship grew between the bold conquistador and the thoughtful, intelligent Aztec ruler.

Once, the friendship was nearly shattered. At Montezuma's invitation, Cortés approached the base of the great Aztec temple. He climbed the 114 steps to a platform overlooking the city. There he found flesh and blood smeared over the stone statue of the Aztec god. Cortés, a religious Christian, was shocked.

He had not known that in the Aztec culture men and boys captured in battle were carried to that platform. There, beneath an image of the Aztec god, the captives were held down by priests. Their still-beating hearts were cut out by another priest using a holy knife. The priests then rubbed their victims' blood on the mouth of the idol and threw the hearts into a sacred bowl.

Cortés tried to persuade Montezuma to stop the

*Human sacrifice was commonly
practiced upon captured enemies.*

34

sacrifices, but the emperor refused. Never, said Montezuma sadly, should he have shown his most holy temple to the white-skinned stranger.

Montezuma did what he could to make the foreigners welcome in his land. He provided female slaves to wait on them. He gave clothing to the Spanish army. There were gifts of gold for Cortés and all of his men, down to the poorest foot soldier. Still the Spaniards feared their Aztec hosts and did not feel safe. Some of them slept in their armor, their horses saddled and ready for action.

Cortés became even more alarmed when he learned that Aztec soldiers had attacked his coastal base, Vera Cruz, killing several Spaniards. Almost certainly such attacks against Spanish forces would spread. Trapped inside Tenochtitlán, Cortés realized that he must act quickly and forcefully or he and his men might be killed.

Going at once to Montezuma's palace, he demanded that the emperor return with him to the quarters of the Spanish until all the Aztecs guilty of attacking Vera Cruz were punished. Montezuma protested. Was this the proper way to treat a royal host? But finally he agreed to go with Cortés. With some embarrassment, he announced to his people that he was visiting his Spanish friends of his own free will. He was not their prisoner. After saying that, he was at the mercy of Cortés.

The Spaniards next demanded that the chief who had raided Vera Cruz be brought from the coast to Tenochtitlán for punishment. Again Montezuma agreed. The guilty chief, along with his son and fifteen other chiefs, were brought to the capital. Cortés ordered that they be burned alive immediately. The executions took place in the courtyard of Montezuma's own palace, before the emperor's own eyes. Yet Montezuma did not try to stop it. By then his people were too confused and too afraid to revolt, even after such a shocking act by the Spaniards.

When the killings were over, Cortés apologized to Montezuma. He treated the emperor with great respect. He allowed his prisoner to send and receive private messages. The strange friendship between the two leaders grew even stronger. But the period of peace between the Aztecs and the Spaniards was destined not to last. Soon it was replaced by bloodshed and death.

CHAPTER FIVE

LA NOCHE TRISTE — "THE SAD NIGHT"

It was the Spaniards' greed and their religion, Christianity, that finally caused the Aztec people to rise in anger against them. First, the greedy Europeans melted down gold kept by the Aztecs to honor their ancient gods. Then, the Spanish priests insisted on placing a cross and a statue of the Virgin Mary inside the Aztec temple. At last, the people of Tenochtitlán became so furious that they began preparing to attack the invaders' palace. What could Cortés do? Because he had destroyed his fleet, there was no easy way to escape from Mexico. Nor could he remain much longer in a city whose people seethed in anger against him.

Just then, runners from the coastline brought astonishing news to Montezuma. A Spanish fleet of eighteen ships, commanded by Pánfilo de Narváez, had landed at Vera Cruz. Its mission, the messengers told their emperor, was direct and simple: to find the traitor, Hernando Cortés, and hang him for going beyond the orders of his superior, the governor of Cuba.

*Diego Rivera's depiction of
Cortés's arrival in Vera Cruz.*

The heroic Cuauhtémoc bravely
defended his city from
the attacking conquistadores.

valuable supplies — crossbows, arrows, powder, horses — things Cortés desperately needed.

Cortés began to raid Indian villages. He also began making plans for returning to the capital city, Tenochtitlán. By May 1521, he had managed to have a fleet of ships constructed that could destroy the swift-moving Aztec canoes in the waters surrounding the city.

Ultimately, Cortés and his men were brutally successful in capturing the Aztec capital.

Then he attacked. When the canoes came within range, the Spaniards opened fire with their powerful cannons. Dozens of the flimsy craft were sunk at once. The Spaniards rammed their heavy ships into the swarm of remaining canoes. In minutes, the waters were filled with splintered canoes and drowning Indians. The Spanish soldiers showed no mercy, rapidly firing their crossbows and muskets into the water at crowds of terrified Aztecs who clutched at floating spars or tried to swim to the safety of their city.

By controlling the lake, Cortés was able to cut off the escape routes of the Aztecs and to prevent food and supplies from being brought to them. Slowly, the Spanish leader began to tighten the ring around the city. He launched surprise attacks. He tore down some buildings and burned others. The Spaniards' Tlascalan allies were given permission to eat the bodies of their victims. Still the Aztecs refused to surrender.

Finally, Cortés ordered an all-out attack by land and water. In one day, 40,000 Aztecs were slaughtered, but the Indians fought on. The canals were clogged with bodies. Many drowned or were butchered in the water.

From among the Aztecs in canoes attempting to escape, the Spaniards captured one bearing the royal emblem. The captive was the new Aztec emperor, Cuauhtémoc, only twenty-five years old. Once ashore, face-to-face with Cortés, the emperor bravely asked the

Montezuma's successor,
Emperor Cuauhtémoc.

Spanish leader to kill him with his dagger. Instead, Cortés, hoping to use him afterward as a "figurehead" ruler, embraced the Aztec chief and praised him for his courage. Later, the two leaders sat quietly together to speak of peace and the rebuilding of the once magnificent city.

With the capture of the emperor on August 13, 1521, the battle ended. Some 200,000 Aztecs were dead. But Cortés, with only a handful of men, had achieved his goal. He had conquered Mexico.

After the conquest of Mexico,
Cortés was received in Spain as a hero.

52

CHAPTER SEVEN
THE
CONQUEROR'S
REWARD

In 1522, Emperor Charles V of Spain named Cortés governor, captain general, and chief justice of New Spain. The Spanish rebuilt Tenochtitlán, or "Mexico City." They explored and settled the countryside. They converted the Indians to Christianity. Gradually, however, the temptation of wealth became too much for the conquerors. They seized the lands of the Indians and branded the native people like cattle, with hot irons. The Spaniards turned them into slaves to work the land.

In May 1528, Cortés returned to Spain. The poor boy of Medellín who had left home to seek his fortune received a hero's welcome. He brought with him a treasure in gold, silver, and precious gems. In his train were captured chiefs, along with strange animals, birds, and fruits. As he traveled from town to town on his way to meet Charles V, thousands of cheering Spaniards lined the streets to see him pass.

But then, returning to Mexico once again, his luck turned for the worse. In 1533, he sent expeditions to

Holy Roman Emperor Charles V

54

Baja California at his own expense, leading one voyage himself. There were storms, shipwrecks, and mutinies. The expeditions all failed. By 1539, Cortés was forced to borrow money. He went deeply into debt.

After several years he returned again to Spain. By then, however, there were new heroes. Cortés was a forgotten man. He was ignored at court, received coldly by Charles V. The once great conquistador was old and ill. Much of his fortune was gone. He had no surviving heirs except for a son he had fathered by his Mexican companion, Doña Marina.

After setting out to sea for Mexico once again, Cortés fell ill. Feeling himself close to death, he returned to an estate he owned, near Seville. There, on December 2, 1547, at the age of sixty-three, he died in bed. A few years later his body was moved to Mexico for reburial.

Hernando Cortés conquered and destroyed a magnificent civilization. It was a cruel civilization, but one that had done no harm to Spain. Moreover, although he defeated the Aztecs in the name of Christianity, his principal purpose clearly was to win great wealth for himself in the shortest possible time. To gain his ends, he did not hesitate to kill thousands of Indians and to enslave many times that number.

Great conquerors like Cortés do much to shape the course of history. Restless, they seem driven to move from one triumph to the next. Their courage, their per-

The Castle of Cuesta, in Seville,
Spain, where Cortés died

sistence, and their imagination speed change in human affairs. Sometimes, too, their conquests substitute a higher form of civilization for a less developed one.

Still, history shows that people usually do not wel-

 56

come change when it is forced upon them. Thus, in the Revolution of 1821, which won Mexico its freedom from Spain, Mexican patriots tried to dig up the bones of Cortés and destroy his remains.

Now, nearly five hundred years after his conquest of Mexico, not a single statue stands in that land to the memory of its great conqueror, Hernando Cortés.

IMPORTANT DATES

1485	Hernando Cortés is born in Medellín, Spain.
1492	Columbus discovers America.
1504	Cortés sails to Caribbean port of Santo Domingo as a member of a military expedition.
1511	Cortés assists in the conquest of Cuba.
1519–March 1	Cortés launches a successful attack on the Maya civilization on Yucatán Peninsula.
1519–April	Spanish fleet commanded by Cortés lands at Vera Cruz, Mexico.
1519–November 1	After conquering the Tlascalans and making them his friends, Cortés sets out for Tenochtitlán.
1519–November 8	Montezuma formally welcomes Cortés and his army.
1520–June 30	After defeating the Spanish forces sent to punish him, Cortés returns to Tenochtitlán.
1520–June 30	Montezuma is stoned by his own people and dies.
1520–June 30	*La noche triste*, "the sad night": Spanish forces withdraw from Tenochtitlán, suffering heavy losses.
1521–May 1	Cortés returns to Tenochtitlán with a powerful fleet and army.
1521–August 13	Aztecs surrender; Mexico is conquered.
1522	Emperor Charles V names Cortés governor, captain-general, and chief justice of New Spain.
1528–May	Cortés returns to Spain and receives a hero's welcome.
1533	Cortés explores Baja California.
1547–December 2	Cortés dies at his estate near Seville, Spain. His body is later returned to Mexico.

FOR FURTHER READING

FOR OLDER READERS

Fiske, John. *The Discovery of America*. Boston: Houghton Mifflin, 1892.

Morison, Samuel Eliot. *The European Discovery of America: The Southern Voyages*. New York: Oxford University Press, 1974.

Prescott, William H. *History of the Conquest of Mexico*. New York: Modern Library, 1936.

————. *History of the Conquest of Peru*. New York: Modern Library, 1936.

Richman, Irving Berdine. *The Spanish Conquerors*. New Haven: Yale University Press, 1921.

Wright, Helen, and Samuel Rapport. *The Great Explorers*. New York: Harper, 1957.

FOR MIDDLE READERS

The Age of Exploration. New York: Marshall Cavendish, 1989.

Hunter, Nigel. *The Expeditions of Cortés*. New York: Bookwright Press, 1990.

Larsen, Anita. *Montezuma's Missing Treasure*. New York: Crestwood House, 1992.

Stein, R. Conrad. *Hernando Cortés*. Chicago: Childrens Press, 1991.

Wepman, Dennis. *Hernando Cortés*. New York: Chelsea House, 1986.

Wilkes, John. *Hernando Cortés: Conquistador in Mexico*. Minneapolis: Lerner Publications, 1977

INDEX

ABOUT
THE
AUTHOR

William Jay Jacobs has studied history at Harvard, Yale, and Princeton and holds a doctorate from Columbia. He has held fellowships with the Ford Foundation and the National Endowment for the Humanities and served as a Fulbright Fellow in India. In addition to broad teaching experience in public and private secondary schools, he has taught at Rutgers University, at Hunter College, and at Harvard. Dr. Jacobs presently is Visiting Fellow in the Department of History at Yale.

Among his previous books for young readers are biographies of such diverse personalities as Abraham Lincoln, Eleanor Roosevelt, Edgar Allan Poe, Hannibal, Hitler, and Mother Teresa. His *America's Story* and *History of the United States* are among the nation's most widely used textbooks.

In the Franklin Watts First Book series, he is the author of *Magellan, Cortés, Pizarro, La Salle, Champlain,* and *Coronado*.

L'ECOLE FRANÇAISE

CHICAGO